# Petey the POSTAL TRUCK

Written by
**Neva Tarver**

Illustrated by
**Erin Robbins**

Print information available on the last page.

Rev. date: 03/25/2015

To order additional copies of this book, contact:
Xlibris
1-888-795-4274
www.Xlibris.com
Orders@Xlibris.com

"Let the little children come to Me, and do not forbide them, for such is the kingdom of God."

**LUKE 18:16**

Every morning before his daily run Petey would pray, "Oh lord help me to make it safely through the day to carry Your precious cargo."

It was a beautiful morning, the sun was brightly shining and the wind was softly whispering. Petey prepared himself for his daily delivery. He checked the balance on his tires by slightly jumping. He cleared his throat to check his engine. He batted his wipers to clear his view and flashed his lights to check his vision. Everything was ready for his daily run.

Today was very special delivery. Petey had to go to the drop point for a church bible drive. He pulled up to the dock and the main door opened and out came Bibby, Veno and Carlos. They were responsible for the accountability of all packages to be loaded onto Petey. All packages were carefully packed with a bible and a toy. Petey opened his rear door.

"Everyone load up," Bibby said, you have a long way to go.

Let's get a count, said Carlos. Everyone count as you load into Petey. Package #1 Spain, Package #2 Germany, Package #3 New York, Package #4 Russia, Package #5 India, Package #6 Israel, Package #7 Austria, Package #8 Holland, Package #9 Texas, Package #10 California.

"O.K. everyone, Bibby said, we can't go anywhere until we are buckled up, for safety is very important." Petey asked, "Is everyone ready for takeoff?" Everyone yelled, "We are ready. Petey smoothly took off. As they were riding everyone was talking about how exciting their night was at the church overnight. "We had so much fun last night before they packed us, said Gennie. The choir was there rehearsing for the Christmas musical and they sounded so good. "Yeah, they sung Silent Night, Holy Night, said Austie. "You know we are very special packages to have holy bibles inside of us, said Gennie. Austie said, "Well you heard the teacher last night saying we need the word in us so that's why they put a bible inside of us." She didn't mean it like that, said Gennie, she meant that we should carry the Word of God in our heart." What's the word of God? asked Austie. "The words in His bible, said Gennie. "Oh I see what you mean, said Austie, we have to learn God's word so it will be in our heart."

"Yeah, that's what she meant, said Gennie. I still have in my heart that song, Silent Night, Holy Night. Why was it a silent night? asked Austie. "Because the baby Jesus was born and He is holy and everything was silent the night He was born, said Gennie.

"Hey you guys listen up, said Andy. I was in the 1st and 2nd grade class and the teacher was telling us about Samson. Did you know that Samson was a very strong man and that he killed a lion with his bare hands and ate honey from the lion?" God made him strong."

"Was he strong like superman, asked Teddy." He was stronger than superman because he had God power. He made a BIG mistake. He gave away the secret that made him strong. That woman name Deliah tricked him and he told her that God made him strong through his hair."

"Through his hair, said Andy, how can hair make him strong?" Did he twist it together hard to make his brain tell him he is strong? "No, No, said Teddy, God gave him power because he had something for him to do so he needed to be strong. So Deliah had his 7 locks of hair shaved from his head and he lost his power." Did he get it back? asked Andy.

"Yes, for a little while. He prayed and asked God to give him power one more time and God did too. So Samson pushed two big poles and made the house fall down." AWESOME, said everyone.

"Only God has the power to do that, said Teddy." He didn't listen to God, said Andy, always listen to God He even tells our mom and dad what to do." WOW!! Mom and dad have to listen to God just like we have to listen to them, COOL."

"Where were you last night?" asked Holley.

"I was in the kinder class and the teacher was telling us about Daniel in the lion's den. Do you know Daniel prayed to God three times a day even when the king said not to," said Micah.

"Did he get in trouble?" asked Holley.

"Well kinda sorta, said Micah, the king threw him in the lion's den but God sent an angel to shut the lion's mouth so they couldn't eat Daniel. So the king went early in the morning to check on Daniel and found that he was still alive. Daniel told the king that God sent an angel to shut the lion's mouth because he did not do anything wrong. I am glad God shut the lions mouth because Daniel was too old to run. He was 80 years old that's almost as old as my dad."

WOW, said everyone. "Don't WOW yet, said Micah, God even let Daniel sleep on the lions for a pillow." A pillow, I want a lion pillow, said Holley." You can't have a real one like Daniel, said Micah. "Well, that's O.K. because I would be scared of a real lion."

"Not if God is with you because if God is with you there is no reason to be scared, said Micah."

"Even when the lights are out?" asked Holley.

"Even when the lights are out," said Micah.

"Where were you packed Onie?" asked Joey.

"I was in the youth class and they played a video where kids were at a rally worshipping Jesus."

"hat's a rally?" asked Joey.

"Well like we all here together talking about Jesus except it is more people and some music."

"We don't have music," said everyone.

"You don't have to, you can make music in your heart," said Onie.

"WHAT", said everyone.

"Put your hand over your heart", said Onie.

"Where is my heart?" asked Holley.

"On the left side of your chest. Now put your hand there and feel the beat." (feeling the heart beat)

"Can you feel it?" "Yes," everyone yelled.

"I want to go to a rally," said Holley.

"We can have one here," said Onie.

We can all worship and praise Jesus right here inside Petey, right Petey? Petey toots his horn BEEP! BEEP!

"How do we worship?" Joey asked.

"Well you think about Jesus and all he has done for you and you honor Him in your heart and with your mouth," said Onie.

"He saved me from a spanking," said Joey. I knew what I did was wrong but my mom said I will let you slide this time. WHEW! That was close, I thanked God too.

"Can we worship now?" the others asked."

"Yes", said Onie. "I will sing and you repeat after me until you get it and then we will all sing together."

"Come into our hearts sweet Jesus we praise Your wonderful name, come into our hearts sweet Jesus for we will never be the same." "Let's worship everybody", said Onie.

They all begin singing. "Come into our hearts sweet Jesus we praise your wonderful name come into our hearts sweet Jesus for we will never be the same. (Repeat 2 times)

"**D**o you feel it?" asked Joey.

"Feel what?" asked everyone.

"That warm feeling like when mom and dad tuck me into bed at night," Onie said.

"I feel that warm feeling like when grandma bakes some good cookies," said Joey.

"I feel that feeling I get when dad and I are on the lake catching fish. I love spending time with my dad," said Austie.

Petey asked, "Do you know what that warm feeling is everyone?"

"No," they said.

"It is the love of Jesus," said Petey.

"The love of Jesus," everyone said. Let's sing it again.

"Come into our hearts sweet Jesus we praise Your wonderful name, come into our hearts sweet Jesus for we will never be the same."

Joey said, "I love Jesus and I want to tell everyone about Him."

"Me, too." Said everyone.

"O.K. everyone," said Petey. We are here and thank you for the worship it has me ready to go pick up more packages like you. Remember I will miss you and don't forget to tell someone about Jesus."

The packages are unloaded and Petey leaves to go another church to pick up a delivery.

Manufactured by Amazon.ca
Bolton, ON